Looking at Plants
Plants and Life

Sally Morgan

Thameside Press

Distributed in the United States by
Smart Apple Media
1980 Lookout Drive
North Mankato, MN 56003

Text © Sally Morgan 2002
Illustrations by Chris Forsey

Editor: Jean Coppendale
Designer: John Jamieson
Picture researcher: Sally Morgan
Educational consultant: Katie Kitching

ISBN 1-931983-12-7

Library of Congress Control Number:
2002 141334

Printed in Hong Kong

10 9 8 7 6 5 4 3 2 1

Picture acknowledgements:
Front Cover (main) Ecoscene/Alex Bartell;
Title page Papilio/Dennis Johnson; 2,10 (B) & cover
insets Papilio/Robert Pickett; 3, 6 & cover insets
Ecoscene/Peter Currell; 4 Ecoscene/Andrew Brown;
5 (T) Chrysalis Images/Robert Pickett (B) & 31
Papilio/Robert Pickett; 6-7 Ecoscene/Andrew Brown;
7 Ecoscene/Sally Morgan; 8 Ecoscene/Anthony
Harrison; 9 (T) Corbis/Stephen Frink (B) Chrysalis
Images/Robert Pickett; 10 (T) & cover insets Papilio/
J. Warwick; 11 (T) Corbis/Sally Morgan (B)
Ecoscene/Gryniewicz; 12 Ecoscene/Edward Bent;
13 (T) Papilio/Robert Gill (B) Papilio/Paul Franklin;
14 & 30 (T) Ecoscene/Sally Morgan; 15 (T) Ecoscene/
Sally Morgan (B) Ecoscene/Robin Williams; 16 (L)
Ecoscene/Judith Platt (R) Ecoscene/Joy Michaud; 17
(T) & 30 (B) Ecoscene/Joy Michaud; 17 (B) 32 &
cover insets Ecoscene/Peter Currell; 18 Ecoscene/
Christine Osborne; 18-19 Ecoscene/ Cooper;
19 (T) Corbis/Michael S. Yamashita (B)
Ecoscene/John Liddiard; 20 Papilio/
Robert Pickett; 21 Ecoscene/ Sally
Morgan; 22 Ecoscene/Chelmick;
22-23 Still Pictures/Edward Parker;
23 Ecoscene/P.Thompson; 24 Ecoscene/
Andrew Brown; 25 (T) Ecoscene/Wayne
Lawler (B) Papilio/Bryan Knox; 26 & cover
insets Ecoscene/Gryniewicz; 27 (T) Papilio/
Robert Gill (B) Ecoscene/Phillip Colla.

Contents

Words in **bold**
are explained
in the glossary
on page 30.

All sorts of plants

There are many, many different types of plants. The biggest plants are tall trees. The smallest are tiny **algae** that live in water. Some plants live for hundreds of years, but others live for only a few weeks.

The giant sequoia is one of the largest trees in the world. The man standing at the bottom of the tree looks tiny.

Most plants are green and have a **shoot** above ground. The shoot is made up of stems, leaves, and flowers.

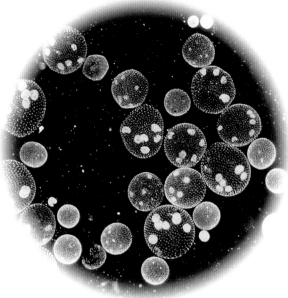

These green circles are tiny plants called algae. They float in water.

flower

Some plants have flowers, and these turn into fruits and seeds.

stem

leaf

This sunflower has a thick stem. The leaves and flower grow out of the stem. The plant also has roots which grow under the ground.

Making food

Plants are different from animals because they can make their own food. This happens in the green leaves. The leaves trap sunlight, which a plant needs to make food. The plant needs water and a gas called carbon dioxide.

Plants have many leaves, to trap as much sunlight as possible.

A potato plant stores food in its underground stems. The ends of the stems grow into potatoes.

underground stem

potato

Plants use their food to grow and to make more plants, or **reproduce**. Some plants store food in their roots and underground stems. They use the food later in the year.

Air to breathe

Plants make a gas called **oxygen**. The plant uses some of the oxygen, but the rest escapes into the air. Oxygen in the air is breathed in by animals. Without plants, there would not be enough oxygen in the air for people and other animals to survive.

When a horse breathes, it takes oxygen into its lungs.

You can see bubbles of oxygen coming off this pond weed.

On a sunny day, you might see bubbles of oxygen coming off water plants in a pond. Water plants put oxygen into the water. Fish and other water animals breathe in the oxygen.

*A tadpole lives in water. It breathes in oxygen through **gills** inside its body .*

Food for animals

Animals eat plants and other animals. Animals which eat only plants are called **herbivores**. Some herbivores eat leaves, while others eat flowers, fruits, or even the roots of plants.

Snails can badly damage a plant by eating all its leaves.

Plants have ways of protecting themselves from herbivores. A few plants are **poisonous** and this stops animals eating the leaves. Some plants are covered in thorns and prickles.

The holly has spiky leaves. The spikes stop animals eating the leaves.

Food chains

Plants are eaten by herbivores. Herbivores are hunted by meat-eating animals, or **carnivores**. This makes a food chain. The plants are always at the bottom of a food chain. Without plants, the animals could not survive.

*Thompson's gazelles are herbivores. They eat grasses on the **savanna** of Africa.*

On the savanna of Africa, grass is eaten by herbivores such as antelope, gazelle, and zebra. These animals are hunted by lions.

Vultures feed on the bodies of any dead animals they find on the savanna.

Vultures quickly spot a dead animal on the savanna. They fly down to feed on the body.

Rotting plants

When plants die, their leaves and stems turn soft. The leaves fall to the ground and rot, or **decay**, quickly. Soon, only a skeleton remains. The **nutrients** in the leaves go back into the soil. Other plants use the nutrients to help them grow.

This leaf has started to decay. The soft parts of the leaf disappear first. The tough bits are left behind as a skeleton.

Dead trees take a long time to rot. A fallen branch or a pile of rotting logs is home to many plants and

*In the fall, clumps of toadstools grow on rotting tree stumps. Toadstools are a type of **fungus**.*

animals. Plants called mosses and ferns grow in the shady spaces. Small animals such as wood lice, millipedes, and centipedes hide beneath the logs.

If you lift up the bark on a rotting log, you may find many small animals, such as these millipedes.

15

Plants as food

Every day, people eat food which is made from plants. Three of the most important plants are wheat, rice, and maize. These plants are large grasses called **cereals**.

The seeds of this wheat plant are ripe and ready to harvest.

Cereal crops are collected in late summer by combine harvesters.

Wheat seeds have a hard outer coat which makes them tough and chewy.

Cereals make seeds which are full of **starch**. Starchy foods give us energy. Wheat seeds are crushed to make flour, which is used to make bread. Rice seeds are cooked in water and eaten, or pounded into flour.

Potatoes are also an important food. They are full of starch, just like cereals.

*Fruits are full of **vitamins** which help to keep people healthy.*

17

Plants as fuel

When wood burns, it gives off lots of heat.
All over the world, people collect firewood
which they burn to make heat for cooking
and hot water. **Charcoal** is wood that has
been slowly roasted in a **furnace**, or oven.

People burn charcoal
on barbecues
to cook food.

*This man has cut small
branches from trees. He will
use the branches as firewood.*

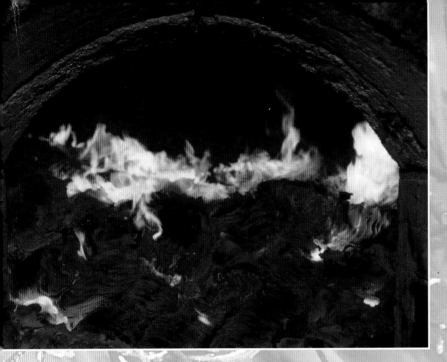

Charcoal is made by burning wood very slowly in a furnace.

Coal and peat are important fuels. They are the remains of plants which died millions of years ago. They are dug from the ground and used in power stations and to make fires.

Peat is dug out of the ground and left to dry. Then it is collected and sold as a fuel.

Plants and water

Plants need water. Their roots take up water from the soil. The water travels through the roots and up the stem to the leaves. Water passes out of the plant through **microscopic** holes in the leaves and escapes into the air as a gas.

The roots of this seedling spread out in the soil so it can take up as much water as possible.

There is not enough water in this plant and its leaves are starting to wither and wilt.

If a plant cannot get enough water, its leaves wilt or go floppy. Eventually the leaves curl up and die.

During a **drought**, plants have to survive many weeks without water. **Cacti** are plants that can live in deserts where there is very little water.

A cactus can survive for months without water.

Where do plants live?

Plants live all over the world, on land and in water. A few plants can even survive on mountain tops and in icy **polar regions**.

Alpine plants live on mountains. They can survive the long, cold winters in the snow.

Forests are places where trees grow close together. The leaves and branches make a canopy or roof over the forest floor. Ferns and mosses live in the shade beneath the trees.

Meadows are fields where grasses and other flowers are left to grow wild.

Grasses grow in meadows and grasslands. **Grazing animals** such as rabbits and horses eat them. Grasses grow from the bottom of their leaves. This means that the plant does not die if an animal eats the tops of the leaves.

In forests, the canopy blocks out most of the light.

Rain forest plants

Tropical rain forests are thick forests in hot and wet places near the **Equator**. The tall trees grow close together. A tiny area of rain forest can be home to thousands of different types of plants.

Palms and ferns grow among the trees in a rain forest. Climbing plants twist round the tree trunks.

This orchid is growing on a tree trunk. The orchid does not harm the tree.

Orchids, ferns, and plants called bromeliads live on the tree branches. Climbing plants called lianas hang like ropes around the trees.

The floor of the rain forest is dark and damp. Palms, ferns, and ginger plants grow here.

This ginger plant can survive in the darkness of the forest floor.

Water plants

Some plants live in wet ground.

Water lilies live in water, but their

leaves float on the surface.

A few plants live beneath

the water surface.

Water lilies grow in ponds, lakes, and streams. Their bright flowers float on the surface.

Seaweeds live in shallow sea water. They do not have proper leaves, stems, and roots. Instead they have fronds, which look like large leaves. At the base of the fronds is a **sucker** called a **holdfast**. This fixes the seaweed to a rock and stops it being washed away.

You can find seaweeds on rocky shores. Their fronds are rubbery and covered in slime.

The giant kelp is the largest type of seaweed. Kelps grow close together, making an underwater forest.

Investigate!

Making oxygen

Plants give off a gas called oxygen. You can't see oxygen coming off plants that live on land. But you can see bubbles of oxygen coming from water plants.

• Place some pondweed in a large, clear plastic bottle.

• Fill the bottle with water and stand it on a sunny windowsill.

Soon you will see tiny bubbles around the leaves. After a while, the bubbles grow larger and rise to the surface.

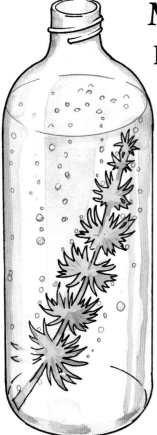

The pondweed produces tiny bubbles of oxygen.

Making colourful flowers

You can use colored water to see how water moves up the stem of a plant.

• Color some water with blue ink and pour it into a vase.

• Take a cut flower with white petals, such as a chrysanthemum or a carnation, and place the stem in the vase.

- Check the flower every half-hour. After a few hours, you will see the color moving into the petals.

This is because the plant sucks water through its stem and into the flower. Then try the experiment again, but use different colored inks.

After a few hours, the petals start to turn blue.

Looking at log piles

A log pile is home to many different plants and animals. You could build a small log pile in a shady corner of a garden.

- Collect logs of different sizes and pile them up. Then you have to wait several months.
- Carefully lift the logs to see what is living in your log pile.

A log pile is home to creatures such as snails, beetles, and centipedes.

Glossary

algae Simple plants that do not have roots, stems, or leaves. Some algae are so small you can only see them under a microscope. Others are huge seaweeds.

cactus (plural **cacti**) A plant that can live in deserts and other dry places.

carnivore An animal that eats other animals.

cereal A grass that has seeds which can be eaten. Wheat, rice, and maize are cereals.

charcoal Wood that has been slightly burned in an oven.

decay To go bad, rot, or break down.

drought A period of time without rain.

Equator An imaginary line that runs around the center of the Earth, halfway between the North and South Poles.

furnace A very hot oven.

fungus (plural **fungi**) Mushrooms and toadstools are fungi. They lack chlorophyll to make their own food and feed on rotting plants.

gill The part of a fish or tadpole that takes in oxygen from water.

grazing animals Animals that eat mostly grasses, such as sheep, deer, and zebra.

herbivore An animal that eats only plants.

holdfast A sticky pad that fixes seaweed to a rock.

microscopic Too small to see without a microscope.

nutrients Substances that plants need for healthy growth.

oxygen A colorless gas in the air. Most plants and animals need oxygen to live.

poisonous Harmful.

polar regions The cold areas around the North Pole and the South Pole.

reproduce To make another living thing.

savanna Flat, grassy land in southern Africa.

shoot The parts of a plant that are above ground, such as the stems, leaves, and flowers.

starch A type of food that a plant stores in its seeds, roots, and underground stems.

sucker A pad that sticks firmly to something.

vitamins Substances that our bodies need in small amounts to stay healthy.

Index